TO MUM

KU-465-707

A gift book
written by children
for mothers everywhere

Edited by
Richard & Helen Exley

Published by Exley Publications Ltd.

To Momtom

Alison Wheeler Age 8

By the same editors:
The Missionary Myth, 1973
Grandmas and Grandpas, 1975
To Dad, 1976
What is a Husband? 1977
Happy Families, 1977
Cats (and other crazy cuddlies), 1978
Dogs (and other funny furries), 1978
Dear World, 1978
A Child's View of Happiness, 1979
A Child's View of Christmas, 1980
What is a baby? 1980
Love, a celebration, 1981
What it's like to be me, 1981

First published 1976
Copyright © Exley Publications Ltd,
12 Ye Corner, Chalk Hill, Watford,
Herts, United Kingdom, WD1 4BS.
ISBN 0 905521 00 5
First printing September 1976
Second printing November 1976
Third printing October 1977
Fourth printing August 1978
Fifth printing August 1980
Sixth printing May 1981
Seventh printing August 1981
Eighth printing August 1982
Ninth printing September 1983

Front cover drawing by Ruth Furber, age 7.
Title page drawing by Lisa Rule, age 9.
Back cover drawing by Annette Nielsen, age 12.
Printed in Hungary by Kossuth Printing House,
Budapest.
All rights reserved. No part of this publication
may be reproduced or transmitted in any form or
by any information storage and retrieval system
without permission in writing from the publisher.

Mothers, mothers, young and old alike, are still as sweet as ever.

Patricia Lentong

Mothers are very special people. Mothers give, and they go on giving irrationally and beyond reason. And anyone who has a special mum likes to say 'thank you', even if somehow they never get down to it. So that's what this book is about. It's a 'thank you' message to every mum from every child.

The entries to this book, and the companion volume TO DAD, have been contributed by nearly 5,000 schoolchildren from all over the world. They come from Britain, the United States, Australia, New Zealand, Trinidad, Jamaica, Denmark, Eire, France, Germany, Holland, Italy, Spain, Switzerland, Cyprus, Egypt, Israel, Turkey, Saudi Arabia, South Africa, India and Nigeria. We are deeply grateful to the dozens of schools which helped in the compilation of the book, and to all the children who made the job so enjoyable. We obviously could not include all the entries, because of space reasons. But we hope that every child will feel that these entries mirror what they felt and wrote. Time and again there were the same stories of how Mum takes such endless care, of how she stays up all night to nurse a sick child, of how she goes on hopeless diets, of how she copes with work, cooking, dad and children. Our task was simply to select the entries that seemed to say these things especially well. Spelling was only corrected where the entry would otherwise have been hard to understand.

As you read the book, remember that *every* picture was drawn by a child, and *every* entry was written by a real child; and if your son or daughter gave you this book they have almost certainly felt most of the sentiments, even if they haven't always said them.

Richard & Helen Exley

Faith Gibbon

3

What is a mum?

Mums are walls which protect their children from the outside world.

Adrian Leto Age 11

Mums are the people who tell you to put wellies on when it is raining, that you need a coat on in a heatwave and that you're still too young to have the radio-control aeroplane that you've wanted since you were three.

William

A mother is a female parent. Somebody to make the beds and wash up. Someone to wake you too early and make you go to bed too early, and some one to see that you *always* do your piano practice.

Susan Age 11

A mum is a woman who buys you sweets and when you have fillings at the dentist she blames you.

Aishling

A mother is a person who lets you stay up late and eat sweets, to get fat and spoty.

Mark Age 10

Mother is a housewife, busy all the day,
Shopping in her lunch hour, running all the way.

Linda Parkinson Age 15

A mum is a person that is always in the right place when you need her.

Claire Bagguely

Mums put plasters on your knee when you fall over and come to see your football match when they don't really want to.

David Champneys Age 10

A mum is supposed to love you and wash boys' smelly socks.

Sally Arthy

Birgitte Nielsen Age 11

A mammy puts up with a lot of things like work and children.

Jennifer McGloin Age 9

A mother is someone some people take for granted.

Paula White Age 13

A mum is a woman who says 'go to bed' and when she says that, you stay very quite and she forgets about you.

Aishling Nolan

A mum is a person who looks after you if you get scared, and if you want your teddy bear.

Elizabeth Bird Age 8

Mums drive you ten times round Norton on Sunday, looking for funny chimney pots to report to the headmaster.

Timothy Robinson Age 12

A mum is a person who lets you creep in beside her to watch the horror film (when Dad is out).

Suzanne Pinder Age 12

Mums are people who are angry when you're at home and sad when you're away.

Vinay Age 12

A mum is someone who always asks you to do something when you're just about to do something else.

Genevieve

Mums have to do all the washing because dads throw their smelly socks arond.

Jacqueline Age 10

A mother is a person who gets married to a man and then she has babies. The baby calls her mother. The baby does the same. She marries when she is older and then she has babies like her mother.

Clara Ortega Age 8

A mother is a lady who finds a man and they reproduce.

Samantha Age 9

Mums wash and dry any dirty rugby kits, five minutes before going to school, having only been given them that morning.

Michael Haworth-Maden Age 12

A mum is not a proper mum if she does not go to bingo two or three times a week.

Andrew Age 13

A mum is someone who always stands up for you when your dad gets cross with you.

Melissa

Lots of mums put lots of Purfume on. Lots of mums have false theeth and Lots of mums have glasses or false eye brows. Mums where wigs to suffocate the nits.

Philip Age 10

A mum is someone who sings in the kitchen.

Elisabeth Fenton Age 12

Mothers are like volcanoes
About muddy puddles on the floor.
Like prehistoric monsters
Like cars screaching
On a wet morning.
Mothers are kind-hearted
Mothers have to be in a hurry
When the door bell goes
The telephone rings
The baby cries
They all start at once.
Some mothers get in a rage
Rushing all over the place
My mother does.

Philip Age 7

Daddy works Mummy Cook

God created mother because he could not be present everywhere.

Taniya Sharma Age 15

Mammy

*Dale Mayers
Age 6*

Multi-purpose mamas

    To a toddler, a mother is an explorer, an astronaut, an indian chief, a cowboy . . . anything that he thinks of as a game.
To an infant, she is a helper, confider, a comforter, even a protector.
When she listens to a junior she always understands and she is always there to tell worries to.

Alison Bain

A mother is a helper
A finder of lost things
A pocket money giver
An angel without wings.

Laura Dalgleish Age 8

    My mum is a Jack of all trades and a master of none. She is a nurse when we are ill, a gardener, a chef, cooks super meals, a waitress, a decorator, a chambermaid, a dressmaker when she makes or knits our clothes, a fruit-picker, a book-keeper when she keeps a budget on her housekeeping, a cleaner, an ironer and most of all she is an Indian (when she's on the warpath).

Julie Age 13

Mildred Calingu Age 7

Leonarda Bochatay

Motherhood

In the Ancient Greek language "mitera" means one who gives life. A mother is the beginning of life. All my family naturally go to my mother when we have any troubles because she is the 'heart' of our home.
Mirto Azina Age 14

A true mother will do everything to make her child happy. She never gets tired of serving. A woman who is privileged to be called mother should honour her calling and be proud of the name.
Merlin Garcia Age 10

Imagine a tower of bricks, the key brick is the very bottom one, for if we take this one out, they all fall down. Our tower is comprised of our ambitions, our hobbies, our hopes and our dreams, with our mother at the bottom. If we take her away, everything crashes down to become broken dreams and fears. Mothers are our making, and if we have a nasty, sarcastic mother we, too, will be like that. If we have a pleasant, happy, generous mother, that is how we turn out.
Sara Robinson

In my opinion a mother loves her children unconditionally.

Paola Benvisto Age 12

Lisa Vassiliades Age 8

Life without them

To all mums everywhere, what would we do without you? Who would do our cleaning and cooking? I certainly wouldn't do it all. What! Wash smelly socks and grubby shirts. Burn my hands in hot, fatty, soapy water, no fear! I'd rather not be born.

Lisa Ollard Age 13

If I had not got a mother my bed would not be done and I would be staying up late watching television. I would all ways be spending my money on things that I would not need. My dinners would probably be a tin of Coke and a cold pork pie and no one would be able to take me out in the car. I would have to do all the house work and so I would not have any spare time. At school I would be a little Dracula and so no one would like me. So I am glad to have a mum.

Michael Jenkins Age 10

Without a mother the household would always be squabbling and there would never be roasts on Sunday.

Jane Moppel Age 12

If it was not for Mum we would look like a sack of potatoes.

Tony Martin Age 12

Karen Barnett Age 9

What would it be like without a mother?
Have you ever thought?
What would it be like to be an orphan?
How would you like to be bought?

So love you mother all you can,
While you have her now.
She won't be there all your life,
So love her all you can, with all you know how.

Sheryl A. Hartley Age 12

In tribute

It is lovely to have a mum. Mums are lovely people and I am going to be a lovely mum when I grow up. I am going to care for my children like my mum and dad cared for me.

Estelle Moreton

My mommy is very nice in side her and very nice outside. Very nice in side means she is not spitful. She is very kind, and very nice on the outsides means she looked beautiful.

Siobhan Age 7

The things my mum does for me are uncountible. She has been helping me hours on end ever since I was born.

Mark Lewis Age 8

I love my mother. She gave birth to me and to her I owe my very being.

Papageorgiou Papakyriacou Zoe Age 15

She laughs when I laugh, she cries when I cry, she lives when I live. I can't say more about her except that she lives for me and I live for her.

Josephides Panayiota Age 16

Mothers do not die because they live in the hearts of their children.

Berna Tahmiscioglu Age 16

Margaret Danou (opposite) Age 8

Funny Mum

They're really very delightful things, always the best in the world, although quite often very silly things.

Stephen

Mummy does not like maniacs who drive on the road. She also does not like alligators or spiders in her bed.

Sean McDonald Age 7

My mum is going to have a baby and she told me that she can't smack me till after April.

Simon Age 10

My mum says, "Yes dear" when she does not know what I am talking about.

Tanya Age 10

The way my mum worries at my exam time anyone would think she was taking them not me.

Robert Booth Age 12

When my mammy talks on the telephone she talks posh.

Hilary Age 7

My mum likes watching old fogies' programmes on television, but she's kind — and that is all that matters.

Rachel Age 11

My mummy calls me her little tweedy-twer-heart and my sister her goosy.

Clare Aldridge

A mum doesn't like travelling at 90 m.ph

Graeme Riddell

17

Mum's like a rugby ball. She gets knocked around a bit, but always stays the same shape.

Mark Age 11

Truely most of the time Mum is a lovable old thing, although she has got a knack for breaking plates, cups etc. quite a lot. And it's only very rarely that she trips up when she's carrying the rubbish bin and the result the most untidy room in Bromley.

Jane Age 13

My mommy gets me round the bend because she once put butter in the washing machine instead of washing powder.

Tracey Age 8

The trouble with mums is that they don't play games though she gives me a few rotten under arm bowls in the summer when I get back from school.

John Age 10

My mummy is sometimes silly and sometimes she is telling jokes. I like it being joked it mackes me laugh.

Samantha Doak Age 7

Mums are funny things!

Mums are sometimes fussy
About manners and being good;
They're always telling boys and girls
About the things they should

Remember when they're out to tea,
Like manners, — 'Do say "please"
And thank the lady nicely when you
know it's time to leave.'

At bath-time there are orders
Like 'Don't forget your feet,
Remember dry yourself quite well
And leave the bathroom neat.

But if ever I was judging,
Then with banners all unfurled,
I'd place a crown upon her head
And vote my mum—'Miss World'.

John Elliott

Adele Cox Age 9

Useful people to have around

A mother usually insists that you learn (or try to) a
musical instrument.
You are taken to an aged piano teacher, and learn that
allegro is a musical term as well as a car.
You learn other things from them too. Nobody lives
on Mars, Mass = Density + volume (or the other way
round?) and not to put your knife in your mouth. In
other words, you start to accumalate a small store of
knowledge.
They are useful people to have around.

David Honigmann Age 9

Some mothers do 'ave 'em

Some mothers do 'ave 'em and my mother's got one.

Michael Haworth·Age 12

If I were my mother, sometimes I would smack me hard.

Diena Lees Age 11

My mum has weird rules that I have to obey, like having a bath, keeping my bedroom tidy and even having my hair cut.

Christopher Moates Age 12

Mum says I'm nicest when I am asleep because I can not say anything wrong.

Richard Age 12

If I were my mother my children would go to bed at 10 o'clock at night and get up at ten in the morning too. They would not have to take VC pills or drink milk of magnesia if they had tummy aches. They would have fifty pence a week plus ten pence VAT. The children would be sent to school once a week just to keep up the good education. When it was a birthday I would not insist on inviting someone like Cecilia Pigface to the party.

Katy Berger Age 11

Mothers always nag at you. I think they should be sold at 10p each for a sort of trick.

Pablo Age 11

The best think I thought Mum did was having me, but others might not think so.

Tim Tripp Age 12

David Age 7

Isn't she a nuisance...

Mums are the sort of people who, before a film starts in the evening, send you to bed saying how awful it will be and then wake you up saying what a fantastic film it was.

Nicholas

I don't like the way my mum puts me to bed. When I am wide awake at night, she makes me go to sleep, and when I'm fast asleep in the morning, she makes me get up!

Stephen

The one problem with my mum is she is allways tidying up, if you put anything down and go away for a minuet when you come back to it, it has been tidyed away.

Ian

John Age 9

Pinickity, pinackity
Lilickety, lilackity
Just like a mother hen
Or even like a mother wren.

It's 'Clean your room!'
Or 'Don't touch the broom'
'Don't eat too fast.
Make your food last'.

P Tucker

Mummy tidys up our rooms and throws my teddy's head away.

Steven

Mothers are funny things really because you never know whether there going to shout at you or not. They say do your bedroom and while your doing your bedroom they tell you to do the stairs and before you know it you have a hole load of jobs to do before your even finished your bedroom. I sometimes wonder where they get them all from.

Heather Age 10

Mums look after you all the time. Trouble is that she looks after you so much that somtimes it becomes annoying.

Judy Age 9

I have never been allowed to stay up and see a Dracula film yet. My mum says I need sleep so I can work hard at school next day, but I think she sends me to bed so she can watch television in peace.

Billie Mayhook Age 13

My mother is strange. One minute she is on my side when I'm fighting with my brother then the next minute she's on his side.

Stephen Shaw Age 10

23

Sean Charlton
Age 8

Twenty one today

When I ask Mum how old she is she always says twenty-one. As I have a sister who is twenty-two even dumb old me knows this cannot be right.

Billie Mayhook Age 13

I think my mum is good looking and so do very many other people. She has dark brown hair and dark brown eyes. You have to give her credit. She is forty-one.

Debbie Age 13

My mother is a teacher and she knows the answers to most questions except what age she is.

Douglas A. Currie Age 13

My mum has been thirty-four for the last three years.

Louise

*Nicola Breakwell
Age 7*

Marrina Age 9

Natter, natter

The habit no mum should be without is nattering over the garden fence; no mum would be complete without it.

Miles Hutchinson Age 10

My mam is quiet but can be gabby at times and one thing she can't stand is been stood out on the street gabbing away, she would much rather sit down and gab over a cuppa.

Dave Age 14

She is always natting on about her and her sister when she was small, I pretend to listen but I watch tele instead. We just say YEH, YEH, YEH. She soon shuts up.

Timothy

My mum is always talking and the only time she is quiet is when she is very interested in what's on television and even then she puts in a quick comment. She is also quiet when she is asleep.

Julie Age 9

James Age 8

Going out

I think my mum is funny because when she plans to go out she has to do her hair, her face and by the time she has finished, it is to late to go out.

Ean Age 10

Every time Mommy goes out to a dance she puts her false nails on, and she looks ever so funny, and Daddy puts aftershave on, and he smells as well.

Elisabeth Age 7

My mother powders her face,
Puts lipstick on,
And cover herself in perfume,
That's why my father disowns her at parties.

Sophia Age 11

My Mummy and daddy going out to the Cinemar

Samantha Goulding Age 8

Andrea Scown Age 7

Mums make you go to the barbers as though you were going to Crufts as a dog.

Peter Wilkinson Age 11

Volker Age 14

Learn. . .or else!

I know she always tries to give what she thinks is best for me — even if that is the hard end of the stick.

Rachel Age 11

Mums are sceptres that hang over you, telling you that you have to get the coal or make your bed. They nag at you, giving you lectures on life in general and how to make your bed in particular.

Peter

Mums should not be allowed to start nagging and the best way to stop her is to keep tidy.

Philippa

My mum smacks me when I am naughty it hurts me very much but I deserve it.

Stephen Age 9

What ever my mum does wrong
I still love her.

Barry Silverman Age 10

Wendy Age 6

Do you know I was born because I wanted to be near my mommy?

Claudia Martinez Age 8

Mum and me

My mum is kind and gentle. Sometimes my mother really loves me and she looks at my face and she smiles at me. I go and sit by her.

Balbinder Kaur Kalsi Age 11

My mummy always makes me happy when I'm sad, when I fall she put plaster on my leg when I get a cut on my leg she cuddles me. She still loves me although I'm very naughty sometimes. When I'm grown up I'm going to be a nice mummy and happy like my mummy.

Leela Salmon Age 9

My Mummy some times calls me Funny names and When I do naughty things and I tell the truth she kisses me.

Mark Grundy Age 6

Alison Baker Age 7

In Mummy's arms

My mother always has room for me in her arms. She's never too busy to give our family the special love a mother can only give.

Donna Jauga Age 9

My mother cares for me. I feel that I've got day and night protection when I'm near her.

Martha van Kees Age 9

Mum is a person you can come to for comfort, when all hope is lost, like an old teddy bear with one eye and half an ear.

Patricia Bowie Age 13

Mums are always busy but never too busy to give you a quick cuddle.

Helen Rankin Age 9

My mum is nice to sit on. She's nice and soft and bouncey.

Paul Fanneaux Age 10

Hadas Nahari Age 9

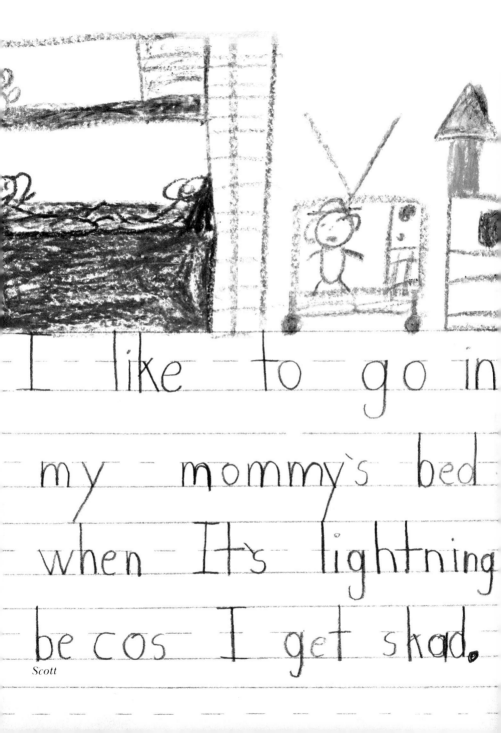

I like to go in
my mommy's bed
when It's lightning
becos I get skad.

Scott

The comforter

Mum is very nice in all sorts of ways. When someone's just bashed you in, you can run to her and she'll comfort you.

Simon Fox Age 10

When ever I hurt myself my mum will go and rescue me, as though I had broken my back when I barely grazed my knee.

Alison Hancock Age 11

Mums always seem to be near when you need them.
When I was six, I used to get very bad ear-ache. One night I could not get to sleep so Mummy stayed up all night until five a.m. when I finally went to sleep. Only then did Mummy go to bed and had to get up at seven thirty to take Penny to school and give Daddy his breakfast. She is a really lovely mother.

Belinda Whitehead Age 11

Bjarne Kalo Age 11

Cooking

When I come home from school, who would be there to make a delicious, warm cup of tea and maybe some hot toasted scones or a quick slap up tea before having a proper dinner. I might have spaghetti bolognaise with a rich luscious trifle, oozing with cream and 'hundreds-and-thousands' sprinkled carefully over the top. Or another night I might have spam and chips with salt and pepper laid over my chips, not forgetting to dribble the tomato sauce over everything. Only a nice, welcoming mum could do that, making the chips how you like them.

Lisa Ollard Age 13

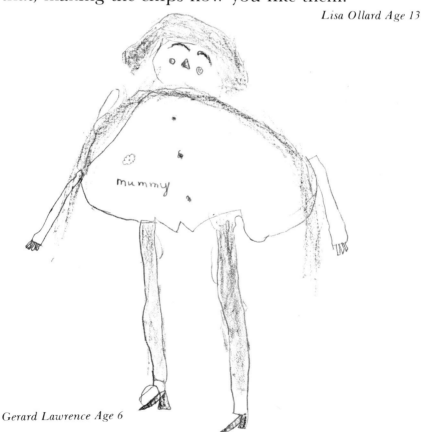

Gerard Lawrence Age 6

Diets

Daddy each day says 'Darling, why don't you eat something. You will be very ill.' Mum gets up every morning at 6 o'clock and eats her diet biscuit, which she says contains a whole breakfast of bacon and eggs. Then poor Mum because she has woken up *so* early, by midday, she gets in a temper! So we all go to a Kentucky Fried Chicken Place, because she is too tired to cook a meal. Well I don't know, I do hope she stops soon.

Wendy Age 13

Mum doesn't have any will-power diet because she isn't very fat and she doesn't have any will-power.

Naral Age 12

Some nights my mum says that she is going to diet. So she cuts down on potatoes, and sugar in her tea. Then we are sitting watching the television she gets through a quarter of sweets! (Or my dad buys some cream cakes) Then my mum says 'I think I'll start my diet tomorrow'. I don't think my mum has ever been on a strict diet in her life but then she would not be the same old cuddly Mum if she was slim.

Jane Age 12

A mother is quite kind at times because if she's having a crafty eat and you go in she gives you something too.

Mark Dowling Age 10

Mum—
Likes antiques
Has even restored some
But hasn't suceeded
With her figure.

Matthew Age 11

Belgin Akyol
Age 13

39

Like a rose

My mother is medium sized, brown in colour and as cool as a cucumber. Her hair is red and thick. She has a proud walk, and is as tender as a chicken. A rose is as beautiful as my mother, and she is as fresh as a daisy, and as strong as an ox.
When I grow up I would like to be as beautiful as my mother. And have the beautiful ways she has. My mother is more precious than gold.

Carmen Ramnath Age 11

My mom is the coolest person in the world. Sometimes she looks like a rose and other times she is just a plain daisy. When she is a rose you can imagine that my mom is very nice.

Wanda Michels Age 11

Mandy Clee Age 10

Abbas Age 8

Mum is always there

When you are ill who is always there,
Quietly sitting stroking your hair?
WHO is always waiting for you to come home?
WHO welcomes you with open arms?
WHO never lets you down?
WHO wakes you up with a lovely smile in the
morning?
WHO's always ready to help?

Vivienne Gilbert

When all other friends have deserted you, Mum is
always here.

Catherine Woodall Age 14

Leslie Johnson Age 6

It's Mum!

When things go wrong
And everything you do goes dong!
Who's always there with smile and help
Comfort, love, or if you need it a scalp?
It's MUM.

We mutter and we mumble and chaff
Because Mum says, 'No it isn't safe!'
But who knows when to pull the rein
Or give the children their way again?
It's MUM.

And when you come home moping, sad
Or maybe just plain hopping mad
Who knows what's best
To sooth the raging in your breast?
It's MUM.

Ian Laurenson Age 11

When we are little children we want Mummy to bring
us sweets, chocolates and toys.
When we are teenagers we want her to understand our
problems.
When we are married we need Mum to help us and to
tell us about many things that we have to know.
In our whole life, we need her, we want something
from her and she never says no!
She gives us everything she owns.

Maria Symeou Age 14

Always a friendly smile,
Always open arms
Willing to help while—
Troubles are at their worst.
The door is always open
To us their children.

Alexandra Hitchings

Elaine Rockley Age 7

Take care of your mum

If you have a mother, give her all your loving care, for you won't know her value, until you see her empty chair.

Mona Fouad El Sakka Age 16

Mums deserve a couple of surprises and treats themselves, for all the hard work they do.

Louise Twaite

With all her worrying about her children, Mother seldom has time to worry about herself. There are, of course, adverts and posters telling parents to take care of their children such as:
'A lesson in life' and
'Under your feet is better than under a car.'
So, why not have posters saying:
'Take care of your Mum, she's valuable' and
'Make sure your parents, Clunk Click Every Trip.'

Alison Bain

Alpoislan Gumundin

Berrin
Suboiy

She's an old softie

A mum is probably the most likley one to give in to you.

Jessica Age 11

I like my mum best because I don't get smacked so much.

Paul Age 8

A mum is someone who will ask Dad if you can go on a school journey, when he has already said no.

Joanne Age 13

Although she seems strict enough
Underneath the skin that's all Bluff.

Samantha Worseldine Age 10

Even the roughest of mothers are very gentle and kind inside, or else they could not be mothers.

Elaine Wong

If I am naughty I always break it to my mum first.

David Age 12

Whenever she gets upset she expresses her feelings angrily, but afterwards she is sorry about the harsh things she said and gives us cookies to show us she loves us.

Avery Age 15

My mum is a bit stupid because every time I ask for something she buy's it me.

Debbie Age 10

I have a super mother who makes cakes, puts them in the pantry and doesn't notice when I eat them.

Mark Wickham-Jones Age 13

A mother never likes to scold her children even though she knows she has to.

Julia Macdonald-Smith Age 13

46

Marilyn Norman Age 8

Kenneth

My mam isn't really
a beauty queen, but
in my heart she is
the prettiest woman
in the world.

Ian Age 10

48

Beautiful in her own way

My mom is as beautiful as anyone can be, well maybe not to everyone but always to me.
Now I don't mean always by looks because you learn all that junk from T.V. and books.
But I mean that she has a beauty inside.

Donna Nitte Age 12

My mother is very kind and when she was younger she was very very pretty. Now she is a bit plump but I like her very very much, she seems to be prettier each day. She doesn't know how to cook very well but when she cooks the dinner it seems to have something special about it. When she makes my bed I think she puts something into it, and I don't awake all night.

Conchita Rey Benayas Age 10

My mum's, well, she's beautiful in her own way. She's not exactly Miss World 1976, but you can't just go and draw a picture of her and say 'That's mum'. There's something about her, whether it's her willingness to listen or what I don't know. But I'm glad she's my mum.

Daryl Mitchell

49

A slave to her family

My mum has not got any hobbies I suppose her hobbey is cleaning the house.

Craig Age 9

A mother's place is in the home, but my mum doesn't think so.

Darren Age 11

My mother gets up between six and halfpast a.m. and she does some general housework and makes breakfast. At seven she wakes up my two brothers and they all have breakfast. Then Mummy gets the boys ready for school, wakes up Daddy, and at quarter to eight she goes off to work.

Joanna Blake Age 11

'What's for supper Mum!'

I see my mum a standing against the kitchen sink,
Scrubbing dishes one by one with wrinkled hands all covered with soap.
Michael yelling all the time makes Mum go round the bend.
Making breckfast, dinners, teas.
Mum, when work is nearly done
Hears the fearful cry again
'What's for supper Mum!!!'

Julie

M for Marriage
U for Unending Work
M for Many blisters

Mark Stevenson Age 12

Richard Adams

Who would want to be a mother?

Everyday you clean the house listening to Tony Blackburn on the radio while you sweep, dust and polish, making our beds, scorching your hands in the washing up, or trying to make the old washing machine work. When all the cleaning's done you can have a rest with a snack and last month's paper which you still have not read. Then there is the shopping and hurry back to have tea ready. Homework comes next. 'Mummy how do you do this' or 'Mummy how do you do that'. After supper, Mum's favorite programme comes on, but of course you have to do the washing up, darn Dad's socks, or sew buttons on school shirts. When she has finished all she is fit for is bed.

Perhaps I do not really want to be a mother after all.

Susan Godfrey

Nicolas Bork Mann Age 14

Poor Mum!

My mother is very patient. She would have to be with five kids, four dogs and two jobs.

Pam Repec Age 12

I sometimes think that they are bossy and bad-tempered but when I think about it I realise how hard it is to be a mum. It is make breakfast, wash up, go shopping, cook dinner, wash up, put feet up, collect the kids from school. I can see why they ask you to wash up or get your own tea. I begin to wonder why they ever become mothers in the first place.

Alan Age 15

My Mum
Christmas
shopping

Maxine Howitt Age 10

Mother dear, you seem tired.
Here, let me stir that pan.
What time did you rise this morning?
At six you say! I don't know how you can!
Do stop a minute, you've been working hard.

You do this every day? Oh Mum!
No, no, I'll wash the sprouts.
Do you enjoy doing this?
Maybe, I have my doubts.
Now just a minute, you've been working hard.

Mind the milk it's boiling over!
I can't believe it! You cook and sew
And rise at six and bed at one
And you enjoy being mother! Oh,
Oh Mum!

Sally Hodder

My mum she works so very hard.
She must be near to tears,
Cos' gimie, gimie! More, More!
Are the only words she hears.

She only wants the magic word,
Oh by the way it's PLEASE
She acts just like a servant,
But never asks for fees.

Susan Harvie Age 10

Petra Hammond Age 9

Temper, temper

On a whole we all love her, except those times when she wallops us.

Robin Age 12

She gets mad when all of us done something bad on the same day, and that's the time when you shouldn't bother her too much.

Juanita

When my mum's angry she is like a two ton lorry going down hill.

Martin Age 10

She Sometimes gets mad and once She got So mad that She made us make our own Breakfast.

Mark Age 9

Sometimes mum's can be dangerous like dragging you out of the room by your hair, or the famous clip round the ear.

Paul Age 9

My mum is very kind and helpful, but she has her bad times bang crash wallop ouch!

John Age 9

Our mum doesn't often spank us but when she does, she does.

Surjit Age 11

Mum gets up at 7.30 am and begins her routine day of housework, headaches, and yelling.

Mark Age 13

I think your mother still loves you even when she shouts and raves at you.

Amanda Age 10

Thank you

My mother is so kind I do not no how to thank Mum. How can I thank you my Mum?

David Webb Age 9

Mother, at every difficult moment in my life I turn to you. You are the only person who can help me whenever I need help, the only person who can make a sacrifice for me. That will be understood only by children who have lost their mothers.

Savva Evangelia Age 17

Who do you go to when
You're in a mess?
Who do you turn to when
You're in distress?

Who gives you money
When you are flat broke?
Who explains why you're late
When you're out with a bloke?

Of course its your mother
Who else could it be?
Give her a treat sometimes
Perhaps make the tea.

Caroline de Silva Age 9

Remember her birthday
And Mother's Day too
You look after her
And she'll look after you!

Debbie Russell Age 16

Mother, I will remember your sweet face for ever. Never will I forget anything you did for me.

Savva Evangelia Age 17

To a very special 'Mother'

This verse is just meant to be, a very special way of saying, 'Thank you, Mother'.

It isn't easy to express the things I want to say,
For what goes on unnoticed, every single day.
But still you are there, with all your understanding heart
And those never-to-be-forgotten words of advice
Which in the end it brought me joy complete.
So Mum, and all others, a tribute to you,
For you are truly the 'Queens' of the world.
(P.S. Don't be a bit worried, Dad, because you aren't so bad.)

Jesse O'Neill Age 13

Iris Harcel

A tribute to my mum

There are four children including me, all girls, and although my mum does two part time cleaning jobs, and runs the home, she always has time to help us, to teach us things, to make us things and to cuddle us all every day.

We are all very close to our mum. I think we are unusually close, because I see my mum do things for us that I think other mums wouldn't bother to do. Mum goes around at night to us and we have a little chat about things. Although my mum believes in strictness we can always talk to our mum about any problems we have.

When I grow up, I will always remember my childhood with great happiness. I never ever want to leave mum. She said we will grow up and have our own children one day. I can only hope I can be as unselfish with my own children as my mum is.

Donna Banyard Age 11

A mother is a person at has babies becaues her is kind.

Gabrielle Age 9

Lessons in life

A good mother is worth a hundred schoolmistresses. The schoolmistress teaches lessons from books while the good mother teaches everything that is useful in life.

Mona Fouad El Sakka Age 16

When I cried, I remember my mother used to tell me how to overcome sadness. She explained to me that the world is full of evil, and if I didn't learn to be strong I would fail. And when she knew I was strong enough to face reality she began to teach me how to find my way in life. She told me that I must learn to be kind, to be a good friend, and always to be ready to help. But I think the most important thing I learnt was to trust myself. It gave me a lot of confidence. My parents gave me the basic values I needed, and because they taught me how to learn, I learnt all the other things by myself. And for that I thank them and love them.

Michal Arlosoroff Age 17

A home with a good mother is the best of schools. There the child learns the lessons of cheerfulness, patience, self-control and the spirit of service.

Mona Fouad El Sakka Age 16

Jessica Gould

A mother is...

A mother is a person who lives her childhood with her children again and is a friend of her children when they grow up.

Isil Ozanogullari Age 17

A mother is a loving angel. Between her arms you find warmth and love which you can never find anywhere else.

Shahira Yossef Age 16

A mother is a person that cares for you, getting out of her hot cosy bed in the middle of the night, giving you milk, when she could have slept on, and not bothered.

Brid Ni Chonghoile Age 14

A mother is a person who loves her children even when she smacks us.

Roger Age 8

Jesper Tønnesen Age 8

Sarah Cakebread Age 10

Kim Bernabe Age 7

Eugenia Escribano

Tony Lynn Age 10

Rupa Age 8

Andrew Green

Lars Age 8

Mother is kind today.
Mother was kind yesterday.
Mother is kind every day.
Mother makes kindness.

Daniel Bajnath Age 10

A watchful eye, a gentle touch,
That happy laugh we love so much,
In every home, there is no other,
Who loves and cares just like a mother.

Gabrielle Smylie Age 12

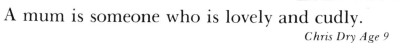

A mum is someone who is lovely and cudly.

Chris Dry Age 9

Mums are really groovey. Helping us when we are sick. Washing, drying, all the lot. Mums are hard working ladies busy here, busy there, busy nearly everywhere.

Ruth Shaw

Mother . . . That was the first word that I learned when I was little. And she was the first person I knew and loved.

Berna Tahmiscioglu Age 16

A mother's worry never ends for her children.

Sheryl A Hartley Age 12

A mother's smile can give you a little happyness when your sad.

Amanda Davey Age 10

Mother is a special gift, that God has given to me.

Rookminee Chatergoon Age 11

'Mum' is the only word that makes everybody all over the world happy, the symbol of devotion. She gives everything that she has, sometimes even her life, for her children without hesitating a moment.

Hasan Ali Tolgay Age 17

Mums have a heart with a key; they open it and love pours out.

Marcia Age 9

Claire Mullan Age 9

Other gift books from Exley Publications

To Dad, £3.95. A gorgeous book for dads, entirely written by children. They've got him taped, too: "A dad is someone who says he will do something sometime, but the time never comes"; "Dads are like moving banks"; "Dads drive too fast and get Summuneds". A heart-warming book, beautifully illustrated in colour. Dad will love it.

What is a Wife? £3.95. A book for those contemplating, enjoying or enduring marriage, compiled from the entries of several thousand ordinary people. The book is a mixture of fun, outraged anger, ribald jokes, and coming through it all, a great deal of love.

Love, a celebration, £4.95. Writers and poets old and new have captured the feeling of being in love in this very personal collection. Some of the best love messages of all ages are sensitively illustrated with fine photograms and grey screened photographs. And to enhance the collection the book is bound in a rich wine-red suedel cloth and finished with gold tooling, gift wrapped and sealed with wax. This is our best-selling book – it makes an ideal love-gift.

Is There Life After Housework? £5.95. A revolutionary book which sets out to show how you can save up to 75% of the time you now spend on cleaning. It is written by a man who heads one of the largest cleaning firms in the world. Humorous illustrations throughout. It's a natural gift to the hardpressed and downtrodden!

Old is . . . great! £3.25. A wicked book of cartoons which pokes fun at youth and revels in the first grey hairs of middle age. 'Extremely funny' *(Daily Telegraph)*.

Grandmas and Grandpas, £3.95. Children are close to grandparents, and this book of children's sayings reflects that warmth. 'Your granny loves you, no matter what you do', 'A grandma is old on the outside but young on the inside'; 'A granny is jolly and when she laughs a warmness spreads over you.' This is a very, very popular book, which makes a particularly loving present for grandparents.

Free Stuff for Kids, £4.50. This book will bring a lot of fun to children aged six to thirteen. There are so many things to write for from the Post Office, Nestlé, PG Tips, Kodak, Longleat, Stanley Gibbons, the RSPB and dozens upon dozens of other firms and organizations. And they're all either free or up to £1. The book is educational too – it teaches children to write and receive letters, and gets them involved in creative hobbies. A very special present, full of potential activity.

The Cook's Lifeline, £4.95 (paperback), £9.95 (hardback). Everything the cook needs for the kitchen and where to get it by post. Food, kitchenware, electrical goods, tiling, floors, lighting, storage jars and so forth. A must for the house-proud or the keen cook.

Free catalogue available on request. Books may be ordered through your bookshop, or by post from Exley Publications, Dept. MUM1, 16 Chalk Hill, Watford, Herts, United Kingdom WD1 4BN. Please add 15p in the £ as a contribution to postage and packing.